Anc ot Gems and Jewels

Created and illustrated by

Alda Marian Jangl
and
James Francis Jangl

ISBN 0-942647-00-9

1st Printing, March 1985
2nd Printing, June 1985
3rd Printing, July 1986
4th Printing, March 1987
5th Printing, August 1989

Other booklets by Prisma Press:

ANCIENT LEGENDS OF HEALING HERBS
ANCIENT LEGENDS OF THE TWELVE BIRTHFLOWERS
THE BIRTHSTONE COLORING BOOK

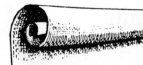

CONTENTS

INTRODUCTION

The love of precious stones is deeply implanted in the human heart. Each one has its own history and mystery, and in every civilization, they have conjured up images of beauty, love, health, power, and protection. They have taken center stage in sacred ceremonies and were treasured by some of the greatest rulers in history. They have been used to fight off all forms of evil, and to heal the afflicted. Their worth was tied more closely to these ennobling qualities than to their monetary value.

History abounds with the use of precious gems in worship. This is because the most valuable and elegant objects have always been chosen for sacred purposes. In fact, there are over 1,700 references to gemstones in the Bible! Probably the most well known religious use of gems is the Breastplate of the High Priest. In the wilderness, God gave Moses instructions for making the vestments of Aaron, the High Priest of Israel. The Breastplate of Judgement as it was called, was to be worn over the chest and set with twelve precious stones, each one engraved with the name of one of the twelve tribes of Israel. The importance of precious gems did not lessen with time, and in Saint John's book of Revelation in the New Testament, the New Jerusalem had twelve stones laid in its foundation.

Most western historians agree that Saint Jerome, a great Father of the Catholic Church, laid the groundwork for what became the custom of wearing a special stone for a given month of birth. In modern times, we marvel at this and other stories that survived to the present day and we wonder: Can carnelian bring good luck? Can one actually see the future by

gazing into a crystal ball made of clear quartz? Did the alchemists change lead into gold? Is it possible to use a gem for healing purposes? Both ancient and modern history indicate that most people of the past would answer yes to these questions.

Oriental writings on gemology link the special qualities of gems with ancient religious practices in the east. Sanskirt writings believed to be thousands of years older than the Dead Sea Scrolls reveal the supernatural attributes of stones and explain how auspicious gems help remove obstructions in various areas of life. These beliefs still exert a powerful influence on the people today.

The Vedic texts tell an interesting story of the dragon, Vala. It begins with Vala's conquest of the Kingdom of Heaven. He thus becomes a tyrannical ruler of the Universe, but the demigods oppose his rule and seek to destroy him. They trick Vala into pretending to be a sacrificial animal in a ritual ceremony. Once the dragon is tied to the stake, the demigods kill him. As they sever the parts of his body, these are magically transformed into precious gem seeds. But suddenly, Vala lets out a thunderous roar which resounds throughout the Heavens. The demigods rush to gather the gem seeds but it is too late, they have scattered. Some fall into rivers, some into oceans, and some into forests and mountains. As they lie buried, they begin to germinate into ruby, sapphire, cat's eye, jade, quartz, and an endless variety of other precious materials. This is the timeless legend of the origin of gemstones.

In the following pages, information from manuscripts, legends, folklore and rituals have been pieced together to preserve the rich romance of precious gems. Experience for yourself the irresistible appeal of these gems as they reflect man's deepest emotions and desires.

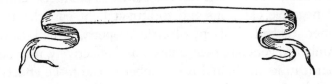

AGATE

Among the many powers attributed to Agate, the most significant was its ability to give a sense of complete acceptance of circumstances. Thus, according to legend, Agate helped a person feel heartened, consoled and strengthened despite many hardships in life.

Agate was named after the river Achates in Sicily because, according to the Greek scientist Theophrastus, the stone was originally found there. The ancient mystics believed that Agate's unusual band-like patterns resembled the spiritual eye. It was thought to banish fear and to protect children from mental illness. Another legend says that any person who looks upon an Agate cannot remain secretive and is compelled to tell the truth. Today Agate symbolizes the love of that which is noble and good.

AMBER

Legend says that long ago, pieces of the sun broke off as it set into the ocean. When they cooled, they formed chunks of Amber, "The Gold of the Sea." It is actually the fossilized resin from a species of extinct pine tree.

The Greek name for Amber was a word meaning "electron." This stone has the ability to produce a charge of negative electrons and to attract light particles to it when rubbed. This pyrolectric property, which causes Amber to generate heat quickly and effectively, may be a factor in its medicinal use. Amber is said to be effective in relieving sore throats and minor infections.

The ancients believed that Amber was formed when pieces of the sun fell into the ocean.

AMETHYST

Amethyst is the most beautiful and valuable form of quartz. The word Amethyst stems from a Greek word meaning "without drunkenness," for in ancient times it was believed that anyone carrying or wearing this stone could not become intoxicated. Perhaps the Greeks were aware of the soothing effect of its rich, purple color, for they believed it had the ability to help control the temperament.

The 7th stone which the sage Iachus gave to Appolonius, Amethyst represented piety and dignity. The early Rosicrucians saw the stone as an emblem of divine sacrifice, since the color was considered a sign of suffering, passion and hope.

The legend of Amethyst is the source of many of the healing qualities which have come to be identified with the stone. The story goes like this. The god Bacchus had been particularly offended one day due to a lack of consideration which he felt he deserved. To appease his anger, he was determined to kill, by means of his tigers, the first person he met. The unfortunate one was Amethyst, a beautiful young maiden who, as fate would have it, crossed his path on her way to worship the goddess Diana at the temple. As the tigers sprang upon her, she pleaded for protection from Diana, who transformed her into a pure, clear stone. Witnessing this miracle and repenting of his crime, Bacchus sought to soothe Amethyst by pouring the juice of the grape over her, bestowing on her a lovely purple hue.

Amethyst is often referred to as the "Bishop's Stone" because a ring set with this gem is still worn today by the Bishops of the Catholic Church, symbolizing their moral victory over worldly passions.

Bacchus colored Amethyst purple by pouring wine over the stone.

AQUAMARINE

Aquamarine received its name from the Latin word for sea water. It is the favored gem of sailors and those who love the ocean. Its cool, light color relaxes the body and is reputed to banish fears and phobias.

During the Middle Ages, it was believed that if a person held an Aquamarine in his mouth, he could call the devil from hell and receive answers to any questions he asked. In modern lore, Aquamarine is the stone of genies, who promise to give those who wear it whatever they wish for.

AZURITE

In both Atlantis and ancient Egypt, it was believed that Azurite was the most potent of all gemstones used for mystical purposes. Its purported psychic powers are now shrouded in mystery, possibly because they were kept secret by the ancient high priests.

Today, Azurite is worn by many to improve their psychic abilities and to aid in meditation. Some attest to its cleaning and purifying effect, while others believe it heightens visual impulses when held in a relaxed state. Azurite may also be placed on the forehead at bedtime to help clarify dream information.

BLOODSTONE

Bloodstone, a variety of green quartz, has characteristic red spots which look like drops of blood. An age-old legend says that this stone was placed at the foot of the cross, where is received the precious drops of blood which fell from Christ's wounds. The stone, thus endowed with mystical and divine qualities, is said to arrest hemorrhaging from wounds and to stop nose bleeds.

There is another legend attributed to Bloodstone or "heliotrope" as it is sometimes called, that claims it had the power to turn the sun blood-red. Furthermore, the stone was reputed to both cause and predict lightning and thunderstorms. Its use as an oracle was accomplished by placing it outdoors, repeating certain incantations, then watching the sky carefully. If a storm appeared with its accompanying sounds, these were interpreted by the mystics into statements about the future.

CARNELIAN

Even today, Carnelian is worn as a good luck charm in Persia and Arabia, where it is thought to protect against the great sin of envy. This belief is closely linked with the traditional folklore of these countries, which says that Carnelian symbolizes good luck and general contentment with one's station in life.

In the 19th century, the wearing of Carnelian was advised for those whose voice was weak or who were too shy to speak. The stone was reputed to give them boldness so that they could converse well and speak in a clear, straightforward manner.

CHRYSOBERYL

Chrysoberyl is a gemstone with a split personality. First, there are two different types of gem known as Chrysoberyl: Alexandrite and Cat's-eye. Secondly, it is true that each of these has a split nature in itself. The Alexandrite displays shades of green during daylight hours, but turns red when placed under artificial or dim light. The chatoyant effect of Cat's-eye produces a lusterous "eye" which appears in the middle of the stone, thus dividing it in half.

ALEXANDRITE

It is said the Alexandrite was named after Czar of Russia, Alexander II, on whose birthday the gem was supposedly discovered. Interestingly, Alexandrite's color change from green to red corresponds to the colors of the Russian Imperial Guard. The stone, which is said to be "emerald by day and ruby by night," has long been a favorite of the people of Russia, where it is still considered an omen of good luck. Traditionally, the most important Alexandrites have been owned by the Russian royal family, and many are found in antique jewelry today.

CAT'S-EYE

The Cat's-eye form of Chrysoberyl is used by natives of Ceylon (Sri Lanka) as a potent charm against evil spirits. It is acknowledged that the finest Cat's-eye gems, which come from this part of the world, were sold for very high prices as far back as the 1600's. In the Orient, Cat's-eye is revered as a token of good fortune, for it guards the owner's property and protects his health. Other folklore suggests that the gem opens the heart center. In this way, it disposes the wearer to perform charitable works and loving actions.

From the Indian Vedic text, we have an account of the creation of Cat's-eye: "Being arrested and bound by the demigods, the great demon Vala emitted a thunderous war cry. This war cry transformed into the seeds of the gem Cat's-eye. Falling into the sea, these seeds agitated the ocean and produced huge waves which washed them upon the shore of nearby lands. Wherever they settled, they formed mines of shimmering Cat's-eye . . . That terrible war cry of Vala also carried heavenward and impregnated the clouds and the sky. Later, carried to earth by rain and comets, these seeds formed smaller mines of Cat's-eyes in scattered areas."

CHRYSOCOLLA

The powerful healing properties of Chrysocolla were once thought to be so effective that its uses were kept a highly guarded secret by the ancient priesthood. Today, Chrysocolla is worn to improve psychic ability, to stimulate dream recall, and to aid in meditation.

CITRINE

Citrine, a yellow variety of quartz, is the stone of lightheartedness. It is said to lend cheerfulness and hope to an unpleasant situation.

Legend tells us that Citrine was used during Atlantean times as a focal point in energy transmission. It emitted an ultrasound frequency like a laser beam, cutting through dense matter. This beam, applied in conjunction with a form of mind control, acted as a powerful sedative and relaxant to the body. In ancient times, the stone was also thought to cleanse the vibrations in the atmosphere. Because of this, Citrine was believed to help bridge the gaps between the mental, emotional and intuitive selves, thus uniting all aspects of the personality.

Later, people carried the Citrine as a protective talisman. It was considered an aid to the digestive system and was said to eliminate toxins from the body. Therefore, those who wore it were presumably blessed with clear complexions, radiant skin and a happy disposition.

CORAL

According to Plato, children who wear coral about the neck will be protected from disease. This interesting custom persisted throughout the Middle Ages. Coral is really the skeleton of a marine animal and as such, it carries with it the special creative vibrations of the sea. Just as the ocean is the life's blood of the land, so too, Coral is said to aid in the circulation of the body and to enrich the blood.

Unlike red and angelskin Coral, black Coral is said to hold in negativity and the limitations that are present in the mind of the wearer. In the past, it was associated with sorcery and was kept in the Shamans' bag. In Tibet, India and other middle eastern countries, black Coral is still considered a sign of bad luck.

DIAMOND

Known as "The Kind of Gems," Diamond is said to enhance the energies of the body, mind and spirit. It is easily used in conjunction with other stones, as its traditional healing properties are not of a specific nature, but work as amplifiers.

Being the most reflective of all stones, Diamond exposes the ego and all selfish desires, but also reveals the purity and sincerity of the good. St. Hildegard, a religious of the Church who believed in the curative attributes of gems, said that the great virtue of Diamond is feared by the devil, and he is a formidable enemy of the stone. The saint insisted that the brilliance of Diamond magnifies goodness, causing people to resist the devil's power.

In modern times, Diamond is the symbol of romance, for it is reputed to strengthen the bonds of love.

EMERALD

Emerald, the gem of Spring, has traditionally been associated with immortality and incorruptibility. It was the favored stone of Venus who, according to legend, detected the infidelity of lovers by its changing color.

In the Jewish tradition, we are told that God gave King Solomon four precious stones, one of which was Emerald. The four are said to depict mastery over creation, symbolized by the four cardinal points. A 78 carat Emerald discovered in Europe once belonged to a Mongul emperor. Written in Persian on the stone were these words, "He who possesses this charm shall enjoy the special protection of God."

Emerald's soothing green has no doubt contributed to the belief in the curative powers of this precious gem.

Throughout the ages it has been used extensively as an antidote against sickness and evil of all kinds. It is especially noted for its beneficial effect upon the eyes.

THE FAIRY STONE CROSS
(Staurolite)

Thousands of years before Columbus discovered America and ages before the mighty Chief Powhatan and his braves roamed the beautiful foothills of the Blue Ridge Mountains of Virginia, a fairy queen named Titania and her subjects, care-free and happy, were gaily dancing and playing with the woodland nymphs of the forest.

Suddenly one day, a strange messenger from far across the sea arrived in their midst, bearing the sad news of the crucifixion of Christ. When these happy fairy dwellers of the forest heard this awful tragedy, their joyful little hearts became filled with sorrow and they wept bitterly. As their teardrops fell to earth, they crystallized to form the beautiful Fairy Stone Crosses. Ever since Titania and her fairy subjects left this special place, the ground has been covered with these mystifying little stones.

Even today, the moss-laden rocks, the sighing trees, and the mystical landscape in the region where the Fairy Stone Crosses are found make this a truly enchanted place. Now know as Fairy Stone State Park, this is the only region in the world where these natural stone crosses exist.

The three type crosses found are the Saint Andrew, the Maltese and the Roman. It is believed that the Saint Andrew type represents the thief who rebuked Christ and this cross, having ten points, is believed to represent the ten commandments. The Maltese cross, which is more of a square shape, is believed to represent the eight beatitudes of the bible. Most perfect of all three crosses is the Roman, which is believed to represent Christ himself and likewise, having eight points, represents the eight beatitudes. Also, the eight outer points of the crosses and the four inner points represent the twelve apostles.

Those who are fortunate enough to wear the crosses hold them in sacred reverence. Because they are "fashioned by God," people believe that the Fairy Stone Cross will protect them against sickness, accidents and misfortune, and that it will bring love, peace and happiness into their lives.

GARNET

Throughout the ages, Garnet has always been noted for its deep, rich color. Ancient legends state that Garnet could never be hidden, that even under clothing, its glowing light would shine forth. According to traditional beliefs, Noah used the wine-red variety of Garnet to light the Ark. The stone's ability to reveal that which is hidden may be the reason why Garnet was once thought to illuminate the mind so it could see back to past incarnations.

HEMATITE

As far back as ancient Egypt, Hematite was used to reduce inflammation and treat hysteria. In his NATURALIS HISTORIA, the Roman writer Pliny cites Hematite as a powerful talisman that could obtain a favorable response to petitions when the wearer appeared before the king. The stone also procured the positive outcome of lawsuits and judgments. In modern folklore, Hematite is considered a grounding stone, helping to maintain the proper balance of mind, body and spirit.

JADE

The Chinese character "pao" meaning "precious," was originally drawn as a house within which was a symbol for Jade beads. It is apparent from this fact that the Chinese have respected and admired the qualities of Jade even from the earliest times when written characters were first used.

According to Chinese tradition, Jade provided a link between the spiritual and the mundane. As the most revered of gem-stones, it symbolizes the eight highest attainments:

In its smoothness a man recognizes Benevolence.

In its high polish—Knowledge.

In its unbending firmness—Righteousness.

In its modest harmlessness—Virtuous Actions.

In its rarity and spotlessness—Purity.

In the way it exposes every flaw—Ingenuity.

In the way it passes from hand to hand without being soiled—Moral conduct.

And in that when struck, it gives forth a sweet note which floats sharply and distinctly to a distance—Music.

LAPIS LAZULI

Lapis Lazuli is called the ancient Alchemists' "Stone of Heaven." It is said to bestow upon the wearer the gift of strength, self-assurance, and increased sensitivity to higher vibrations.

The special mystical quality associated with Lapis made it sacred to the Egyptians. For a time only the pharaohs, the royal family members, and the priests were permitted to wear it. Accordingly, Egyptian tombs were replete with carvings of Lapis, for it was believed that this stone would protect, guide and cheer the dead as they journeyed into the afterlife.

An ancient legend tells of an eye, fashioned out of Lapis Lazuli and gold, and inscribed with the 140th chapter of the Egyptian Book of the Dead. We are told that on the last day of the month, an offering was made to the god Ra before this symbolic spiritual eye, for on that same day, it was believed, the god placed the Lapis amulet upon his own head.

Another tradition states that the ten commandments which Moses gave the people were carved on two blocks of Lapis Lazuli. This stone was also highly prized in China, where sacred writings reveal its use in offerings made to the Lord of the Universe.

LODESTONE

The dictionary defines Lodestone as "a strongly magnetic variety of the mineral magnetite." Although not a gemstone, this material has been the focus of many interesting legends throughout history.

In several languages, the name given to Lodestone indicates how the power of attraction (which Lodestone displays for iron) is akin to the "magnetic" force of love. In Sanskrit for instance, the name for Lodestone, "chum-baka" means "the kisser," and in Chinese, the name "t'su shi" is literally "the loving stone." An 8th century Chinese writing declares, "The Lodestone attracts iron just as does a tender mother when she calls her children to her."

The theme of love that is associated with Lodestone is documented by such notables as Plato, Pliny, and the 5th century poet Claudian. One story tells of Ptolemy, an Egyptian king who wished to create a statue of his wife, which he intended to place in a temple erected in her honor. The design called for huge blocks of Lodestone to be placed in the floor and roof of the temple in such a way that the iron statue would hang suspended in mid-air. Unfortunately, both the king and his architect died before the plan could be implemented.

Claudian relates how the priests of a certain temple devised a scheme for a magnificent spectacle involving the power of Lodestone. They had two statues made, one of Mars in iron—the god of war, and the other of Venus in Lodestone—the goddess of love. At a special ceremony, the priests arranged the statues a short distance apart. At the appropriate time we are told, Mars flew into Venus' waiting arms.

Further elaborations of the love theme have been carried down through the centuries. There is an old folktale which says that if a husband placed Lodestone under his wife's pillow, it will measure the extent of her virtue. If she be faithful, the stone would cause her to embrace her husband. If not, it would make her jump up in bed in fright.

Lodestone is a conjuror's stone, which is to say, it has been used in Voodoo ceremonies to materialize desires which are spoken or held in the minds of the conjurors. At Magnet Cove, Arkansas, where there is a large deposit of Lodestone, this practice is well known. On the record in Macon, Georgia is a case from 1887 in which a woman sued her conjuror when the Lodestone she bought from him for five dollars failed to bring back her wandering husband. The judge ordered her money refunded.

MALACHITE

The wide use of cosmetics and beauty aids in all the ancient civilizations is quite extraordinary. Malachite was one of those gems which, when pulverized, produced a lovely green eye shadow. From tombs whose origin preceded those of Egypt, we find cosmetic jars and paint cups containing Malachite. Later on, King Solomon extracted this gem as a copper byproduct from his fabulous mines and became wealthy as a result.

In Egypt, Malachite was used primarily as a protection for children against evil spirits. During the Middle Ages, it was a popular talisman against the Evil Eye, all forms of sorcery and black magic.

Modern folklore suggests that Malachite increases abundance in all areas of life, offering its wearer health, vitality and protection.

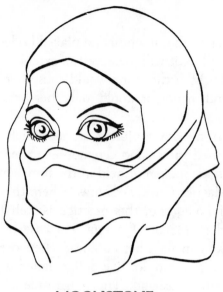

MOONSTONE

Moonstone, a gem of emotion, is said to arouse the tender passions of young lovers. In metaphysical lore, it is noted for its exceptional ability to enable its owner to perceive the future—but only if the stone is carefully placed under the tongue on the night of the full moon!

According to East Indian tradition, Moonstone is the gem which symbolizes the Third Eye. It is said to give clarity to spiritual understanding and to assist those in the astral realm. The Moonstone is never offered for sale in India except when displayed on a yellow cloth, for yellow is considered an especially sacred color, worthy to carry this highly esteemed gemstone.

There is a legend which tells of a wonderful Moonstone owned by Pope Leo X. Dull and lifeless when the moon was old, it grew in brightness as the moon increased in light. Finally, the gem displayed remarkable brilliance when the moon was full. It is said to have consistently waxed and waned each month in synch with the lunar cycle.

ONYX

In ancient times, Onyx was used to guard against witches' spells and evil sorcery. It was reputed to drive away all undesirable thoughts and bad temper. Folklore says that Onyx was considered a stabilizing stone, especially during times of extreme stress because it prevented loss of energy from the body.

In India, another legend states that Onyx was worn around the neck in order to cool the passions of love. It was further believed that the stone encouraged a spirit of separateness and independence between partners.

OPAL

Known as "The Gem of the Gods," Opal has always had a mystical significance. It is said to aid in psychic vision and to have the power to open the spiritual centers. As a curative stone, Opal was believed to heighten weak emotions and to strengthen the memory.

During the time of Queen Elizabeth, Opal was written "ophal." Some believe the name was derived from the word "ophthalmos" meaning, "the eye." Thus, in ancient times, Opal was said to be intimately connected with a belief in the Evil Eye. Over the years, a superstition developed which said the stone caused ill luck if gazed upon. In contrast, another folktale of a later date suggests that looking at Opal is actually good for the eyes.

At one time, this stone was considered the gem of love. Opal could reverse its lucky effects for those who lacked fidelity, however, bestowing unfortunate circumstances upon unfaithful lovers.

PEARL

A lovely Pearl, which results from irritation in the oyster, is symbolic of the mystic's divine purpose of transmutation. The struggle of each human being can be likened to the formation of a Pearl; there is growth from humble beginnings, the attempt at self-preservation through patience and in concealment, until finally a magnificent transformation takes place where the irritant has actually created from itself a most prized possession of true beauty. Thus the Pearl has come to represent the virtues of purity, modesty, and gentleness.

An ancient tale explains that Cleopatra, in an attempt to capture for herself the beauty of Pearl, dissolved one in vinegar and drank it. It is also said that on another occasion, she wagered Marc Anthony that she could swallow the entire value of a province at one meal. With that, she took a perfectly flawless Pearl of enormous value, ground it into a fine powder, placed the powder in a glass of wine and swallowed it.

Throughout history, Pearls have always been a priceless treasure.

PERIDOT

Peridot is a gem variety of olivine, also known as "chrysolite." Highly valued by the ancients, the stones were once considered more valuable than diamonds. In fact, they were actually used as currency to pay tribute to Egyptian rulers. The ancients of that day believed that Peridot could only be found at night, when the stone radiated like the sun. Although it was said to glow, Peridot was never mined at night. Instead, the spot where the light appeared was carefully marked, and the diggers returned the following day to unearth the gems.

Peridot was the only gem set in transparent form by the Romans, who wore it for protection against enchantments, melancholy and illusion. During the Middle Ages, knights wore the stone as a means of gaining foresight and divine inspiration. It was also recommended for those who desired eloquence in speech.

QUARTZ (ROCK CRYSTAL)

Since the earliest days of recorded time, Quartz has been singled out as the magical stone of divination and clairvoyance. Known as "Ice of Eternity" to the Greeks and "The Philosopher's Stone" to the mystics, it is truly unique, for it is capable of dispersing white light into the seven spectral colors.

In addition, natural Quartz has the ability to amplify, bend and synchronize many types of energy such as light, electricity, magnetic fields and even more subtle vibrational patterns which scientists are just beginning to discover. This special piezoelectric property may well be responsible for the reputed power of Quartz to align one's consciousness with the electromagnetic forces of the universe.

Gazing into the crystal is part of a timeless tradition. To explore past and future, to see visions and to gain insights which are normally unavailable to our mental faculties; these mysteries and more have been handed down to us from Celtic legends, Oriental magic, Alchemical romances, and customs based upon ritual. Today we see remnants of these ancient beliefs in our own fables and fairy tales.

Its special shapes and colors make Quartz attractive as well as versatile. Whether it be a single crystal point or one with double termination (Herkimer Diamond), a crystal ball or a pyramid fashioned from rock crystal, the special shape is said to increase the natural power of Quartz itself. Rutilated Quartz has golden rutile needles within the stone which serve to focus the attention. Smoky Quartz is especially good for calming the mind, while the soft color of Rose Quartz is said to promote the vibrations of universal love and inner serenity. Whatever form Quartz may take, it is the stone that was once believed to bring the energy of the stars into the soul of man.

RUBY

Exhibiting the most dynamic of all colors, the Ruby has been aptly dedicated to high noon and bright midsummer. It was thought to contain a glowing spark struck from the planet Mars, a spark that could not be quenched until the world itself grew cold.

Ruby is the Hindu's "King of Precious Stones," and is said to increase vigor, renew vital life forces, and help cleanse the system. Ancient physicians relied on Ruby to treat all afflictions of the circulatory system. It was supposed to stop hemorrhaging and check the flow of blood.

The magnificent color of Ruby is probably the reason why it has been called throughout the centuries, "The Stone of Courage." It was the special gem assigned to the Brahmin caste in India, the highest rank to which a person could belong. The wearer, it was believed, was able to live among evil men without fear of bad fortune. Moreover, the potency of Ruby was such that "even an ignorant person living a sinful life and surrounded by deadly enemies is saved by wearing such a gem."

SAPPHIRE

The ancient Vedic text tells us that, "The eyes of the great demon Vala . . . were transformed into the seeds of blue Sapphire gems and fell down on the sacred land of Sinhala and the surrounding tropical areas of Southeast Asia. These Sapphire seeds fell in such abundance that these lush and beautiful lands glowed with dazzling splendor."

As the gem of Autumn, Sapphire brings to mind the beautiful blue of a September sky. No wonder the Persians believed that the earth rests on a gigantic Sapphire with the celestial heavens reflecting its color!

The calming blue of Sapphire, which has a relaxing effect upon the mind, is said to give one an awareness of cosmic realms. The stone symbolizes clear thinking and is capable of strengthening the will of the person who wears it. Star Sapphire, also called "The Stone of Destiny," has its own particular legend. The three chatoyant bands that form the star represent the virtues of faith, hope and charity.

TIGEREYE

The ancient Romans valued Tigereye as a powerful protective amulet. Soldiers carried it into battle because they believed it gave them quick thinking and a decisive advantage over their adversaries.

Modern folklore says that Tigereye has a "down-to-earth" influence symbolized by its golden earth tones. It is also reputed to bring greater power to the mind and clarify the thought processes.

TOPAZ

Topaz has a long and interesting history; its folktales have been passed down through the ages with many fascinating anecdotes:

To the ancient Egyptians, the golden glow of the Topaz symbolized Ra, the Sun god who was the Giver of Life.

The Greeks called Topaz the "Stone of Strength," and used it extensively for medicinal purposes.

In the Far East, soothsayers believed that with the help of the Topaz, they could contact astral beings, especially during the waxing moon.

In medieval times, Topaz was employed for healing certain illnesses which are particular to women. In addition, it was found to be especially helpful in the treatment of tension headaches and the prevention of bad dreams.

During the Middle Ages, religious faith and a belief in the curative properties of gems came to exist side by side. With Topaz, there are several instances of this. For example, the stone was recommended by St. Hildegard as a cure for weak vision. She suggested that the Topaz be placed in a glass of wine and left for three days and three nights. Before going to sleep each evening, the patient was to rub his eyes with the wine-moistened stone so that the moisture lightly touched the eyeballs. The wine could also be drunk for health purposes after the Topaz had been removed for up to five days.

In the 15th century, a certain Topaz was reputed to have caused miraculous cures. The stone responsible for these healings was greatly revered by the faithful because it had belonged to two popes, Clement VI and Gregory II. Subsequently, the Topaz was acquired by a Roman physician who used it to treat those afflicted with the plague. His reported success was said to be due to the fact that the people placed exceptional faith in the healing powers of the papal stone, and it was this faith that did, in fact, hasten their recovery.

To the Egyptians, the golden glow of Topaz symbolized Ra, the sun god.

TURQUOISE

Tradition says that Isaac, the son of Abraham, was the first to open the famed Persian Turquoise mines. Although various versions of the bible disagree, some scholars believe that the gem was one of the precious stones that comprises the foundation of the New Jerusalem.

In ancient lore, the beautiful blue color of Turquoise represented the atmosphere surrounding the earth, which was regarded as the giver of life and breath. The stone further signified man's origin as a creature of spirit rather than of flesh.

A belief that Turquoise brought good luck was prevalent during the time of Shakespeare. Also, superstitions alluded to the belief that the stone grew pale when its owner took sick and lost its color completely at death. Turquoise would regain its color however, if it was worn by a new and healthy owner.

Today, the American Indian reveres Turquoise for its balancing and healing energy. It is said to act as a unifying force between the Spirit of air and the Spirit of the earth.

ZIRCON

Archaeology indicates that Zircon was one of the earliest, if not the first, of gems used by man. In the bible, the stone is called "jacinth" which is its ancient name. Ironically, the compilers of more recent editions seem to prefer "jacinth," while older translations of the bible refer to the stone as Zircon.

Ancient travelers wore Zircon as an amulet to protect them against the plague, wounds, and injuries. The stone was credited with guarding sailors from lightning and expelling evil spirits by its brightness.

BIRTHSTONE OF THE MONTH

January .Garnet
February . . . . .Amethyst
March. . . . . .Aquamarine or Bloodstone
April . . . . .Diamond
May . . . . .Emerald
June . . . . .Alexandrite or Pearl
July. . . . . .Ruby
August . . . . .Peridot or Onyx
September . . . . .Sapphire
October .Opal
November . . . . .Topaz or Citrine
December. . . . . .Zircon or Turquoise

For information on other books and products from
Prisma Press, please write to:

Prisma Press Publications
P.O. Box 1203
Coeur d'Alene, Idaho 83814

DISCLAIMER

The statements made in this booklet are for information only. We
make no claims as to the therapeutic value of the gems described.